SKETCHING WITH A PENCIL

for those who are
just beginning.

BLANDFORD

Blandford

an imprint of

Cassell

Wellington House, 125 Strand
London WC2R 0BB

Copyright © John Hamilton 1989

First published 1989
This edition 1991
Reprinted 1991, 1992, 1993, 1994, 1995, 1996, 1997, 1999, 2000

British Library Cataloguing in Publication Data
A catalogue record for this book is available from
the British Library

ISBN 0-7137-2284-3

The moral right of the Author has been asserted

Distributed in the United States by
Sterling Publishing Co., Inc.,
387 Park Avenue South
New York, NY 10016-8810

Printed and Bound in Great Britain by
Hillman Printers (Frome) Ltd

I live on the island of Tresco in the Isles of Scilly, and during the year many hundreds of people come to my studio. They are on holiday, relaxing and enjoying the beauty and peace of Tresco. From that relaxation often grows the feeling that they would like to try their hand at sketching. All too often people give up with the words 'I really would love to draw, but I've tried and find that I just can't'.

There are a number of most attractive books on drawing on the market, but with very few exceptions I find that for the complete beginner they are confusing. One of those exceptions is *How to draw* by the late Adrian Hill. So often, they start by listing a whole range of equipment that is used in the book, and then jump too quickly into an area which is beyond the ability of those who really are just beginning. After all, you can increase your tools and include charcoal, pen and ink, crayons, pastels and water colours whenever you feel like it — but for many people the initial hurdle is to start, and having started, to have the confidence to continue.

That is the reason for this little book.

As I said on the previous page, so many people seem to give up drawing almost before they have begun. This is usually because they choose a subject which is too difficult, and not surprisingly they are disheartened by the result. **We** are not going to fall into that trap.

Having said that, let's begin.

Firstly, what equipment should you have?

For your SKETCH BOOK, choose one with a strong cardboard back and some form of spiral binding. A glued binding tends to fall apart with use, and particularly so if it gets wet. As for size, I use an A4 (the same size as this book), but with experience you will find the size that suits you. Stick to that size. A smooth white paper can be found at your art shop, and it will be adequate for your early work. Always include a large BULLDOG clip to stop the paper blowing in the wind, and include a clear plastic 12 inch RULER.

Your PENCILS should be good quality, and I suggest HB, 2B, 4B and 6B. Pencils are graded from 6H which is very hard and is used mostly by draughtsmen, through to 6B which is soft and very black. HB is in the middle. You can always add to your collection at any time, but I want to start you off with the minimum of equipment so as not to confuse you.

You must include a very sharp KNIFE. A Stanley type is ideal, and a pencil sharpener can be included, although it does not give you a long enough point for everything you will want to do. Put a strip of fine sandpaper in your bag. It will be invaluable for sharpening up the point of your pencils.

Include a good RUBBER. The best kind will be very soft and bungy, and large enough not to become lost.

Finally we come to the all-important question of a comfortable STOOL. There are all kinds and sizes on the market, but I went to a fishing tackle shop and found an ideal model. It is light, and has a strap which enables you to carry it from the shoulder and thus have both hands free. However the best thing about it is that it has a waterproof bag attached to the side of the stool, and it carries all my equipment.

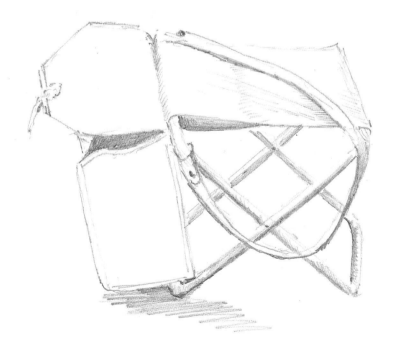

Having chosen your equipment, I want you to try it out. It will be useful to have a small scribbling pad with you.

First take time to sharpen your pencils with long tapering points, and always keep your pencils sharp.

Practise using the pencils like this. It is so basic and so important. Try to have a flexible wrist and relax. Let your whole arm become supple, have a light touch and don't be tensed up in any way.

Now do it again . . .

    and again . . .

    and again . . .

until you are happy with the result
    and feel relaxed.

HB   2B   4B   6B

Do the same thing, but hold the pencil against a ruler, like this

and include a rubber — like this, but always clean your rubber after each stroke, on a spare piece of paper.

Now let's start—but **please remember**—you are not going to try anything that is too difficult at first.

You are sitting in the countryside or on a beach and looking at the scene in front of you, trying to make up your mind what you will draw. Here is a hint. Take the outer box of a match box and put it to your eye. Better still cut a rectangle out of a piece of card.

What you see is the area that will fill your page. Have you ever thought that it is only when your eyes concentrate on a particular tree or wall or bush that you are aware of the intricate detail. Otherwise there is only a general form of landscape. So what you decide to leave out is almost as important as what you put in.

Forget the detail for a moment, and consider where you are going to place the horizon in your first sketch.

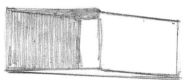

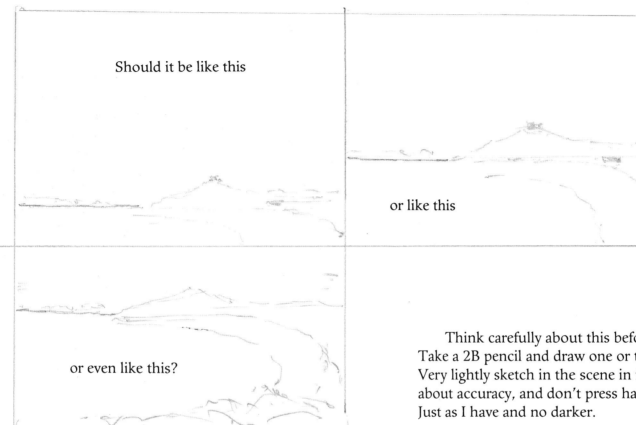

Should it be like this

or like this

or even like this?

Think carefully about this before you start your drawing. Take a 2B pencil and draw one or two rectangles like I have. Very lightly sketch in the scene in front of you. Don't worry about accuracy, and don't press hard. Keep it light and simple. Just as I have and no darker.

Two things are happening. Firstly you are thinking about your composition and the limits of what you can put down on the paper — remembering to look through the frame you made just now, or the match box. Secondly you are relaxing and your wrist and forearm are becoming supple.

You are drawing hardly more than a series of doodles, but you are learning a lot and composing your sketch.

You have decided where to place the horizon—in my case a quarter of the way down from the top of the page. It has gone in lightly with a 2B. In this way I can relate the hill, the castle and the foreground to my line of horizon. It is only in outline, and at this stage we are not trying to produce a masterpiece—just a preliminary thumbnail sketch.

The outline is in and we can now start some shading. There are few rules, but in general the further away into the distance you are, the lighter the shading.

I finished the sketch and ended up using a 4B and a 6B pencil in the foreground. Study carefully what I must have left out. There are no clouds and the sea is untouched. I have tried to make a difference between the islands in the distance and the foreground. We are always striving to give a three dimensional effect to a flat surface. This is not a finished drawing—it is a sketch, and I hope you will have great fun and satisfaction in filling your sketch book with the results of your work.

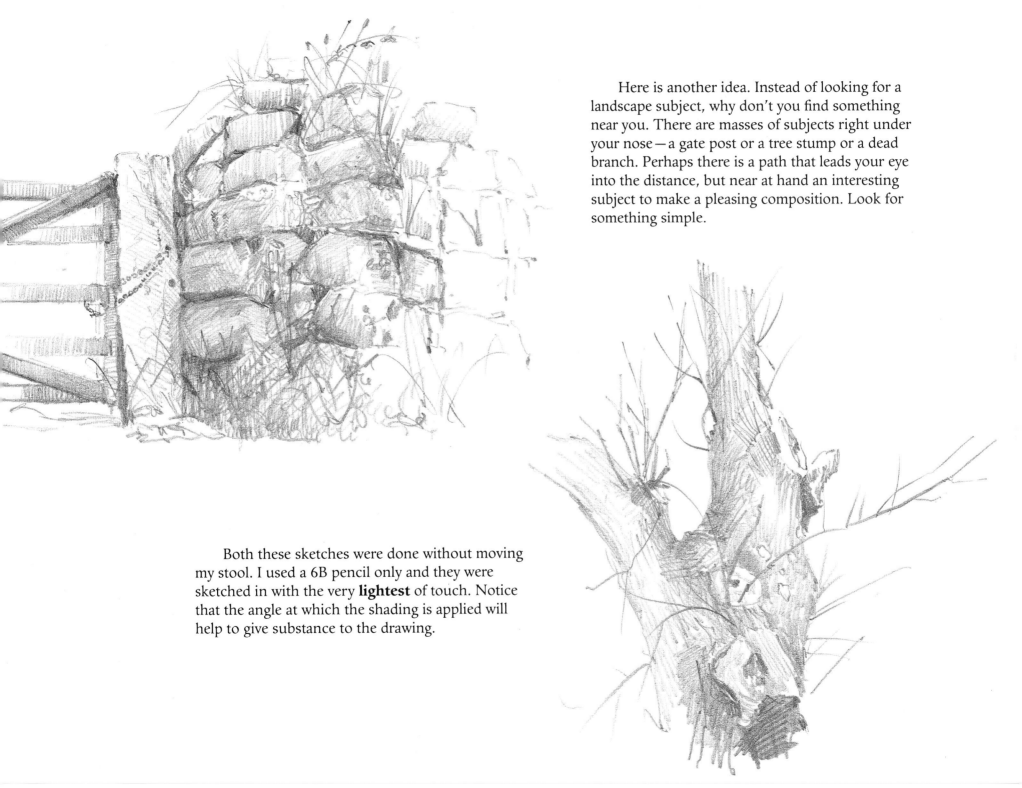

Here is another idea. Instead of looking for a landscape subject, why don't you find something near you. There are masses of subjects right under your nose—a gate post or a tree stump or a dead branch. Perhaps there is a path that leads your eye into the distance, but near at hand an interesting subject to make a pleasing composition. Look for something simple.

Both these sketches were done without moving my stool. I used a 6B pencil only and they were sketched in with the very **lightest** of touch. Notice that the angle at which the shading is applied will help to give substance to the drawing.

It is time to become a little more critical. Study the composition of these two sketches. I didn't have to move very far, but they are both different. In future, I hope that you will be looking at subjects as compositions for a sketch. When you are browsing through your photographs, or indeed when you are about to take a photograph, try to think of compositions. The same is true for reproductions in magazines and books, and when you are looking at a painting. Ask yourself, 'Do I like this composition, or could it be improved?' Now do the same when you are out of doors, and always be on the lookout for a simple but effective composition. When you are considering a subject, move fifty yards to either side and see if the composition is improved. Which part of the scene appeals to you most? In this case, is it the porch or the rose window or the gravestones in the foreground?

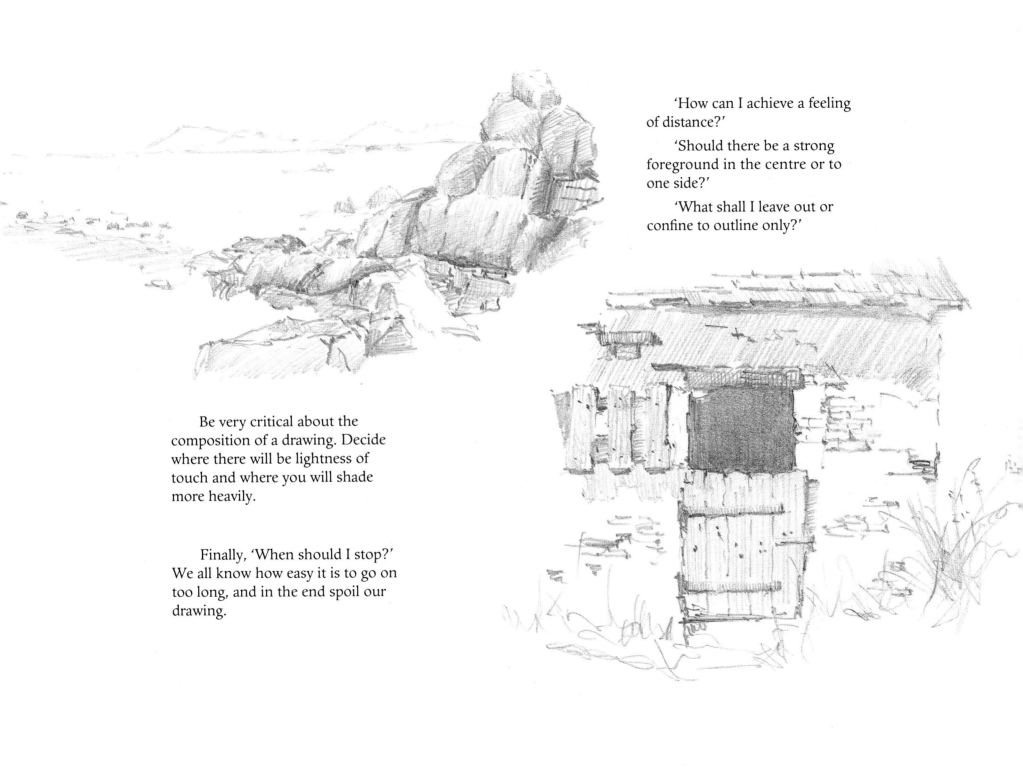

'How can I achieve a feeling of distance?'

'Should there be a strong foreground in the centre or to one side?'

'What shall I leave out or confine to outline only?'

Be very critical about the composition of a drawing. Decide where there will be lightness of touch and where you will shade more heavily.

Finally, 'When should I stop?' We all know how easy it is to go on too long, and in the end spoil our drawing.

If I had drawn the house in detail it would have overshadowed the seat and the old outhouse. Instead, I started by sketching in the main features **very** lightly with a 2B pencil, and then shaded round the seat to bring it forward.

The full strength of my 6B pencil was used round the edge of parts of the seat. Then I tried to give a feeling of separate identity firstly of the seat, then the wall behind it, then the outhouse with its door, and finally the outline of the house.

At this stage I want to introduce you to PERSPECTIVE. It can be a little daunting at first, but I want to suggest some very basic thoughts. Firstly, objects tend to converge and diminish as they recede into the distance. When they actually disappear at the horizon, they are said to have reached the vanishing point. A line of trees or a railway track are good examples of this.

As we have seen, your eye level dictates the position of the horizon. It can be anywhere on a sketch but it will affect your drawing in every way. These three examples show what happens when you are below your subject, and looking up at it; when you are level with it; and when you are above it. Don't be put off by these problems, for it's early days yet. The most important task is to keep confident and enthusiastic about your drawing. I will introduce perspective from time to time — and provided you spend a little time trying to understand that it is a natural part of your drawing, I don't think it will prove too difficult.

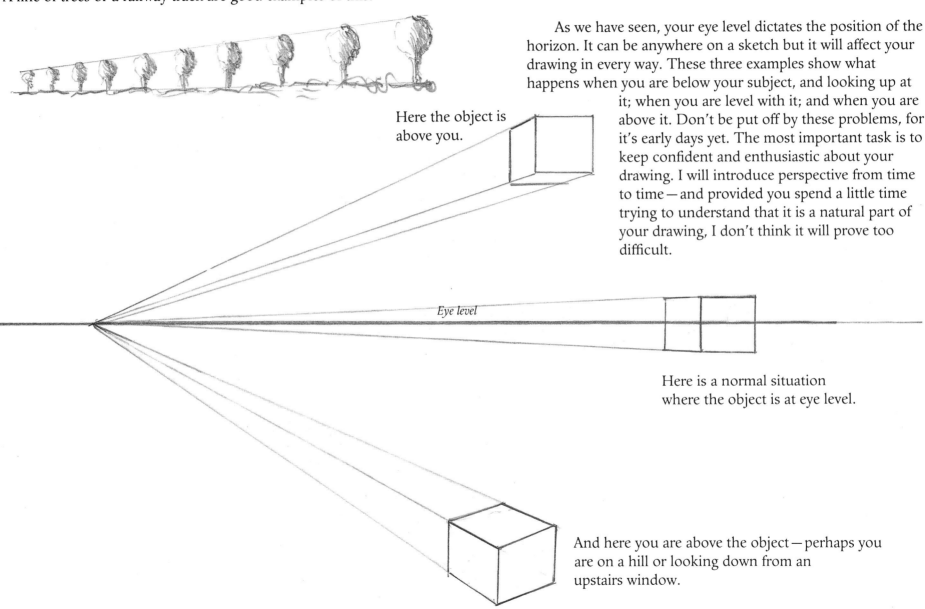

Here the object is above you.

Eye level

Here is a normal situation where the object is at eye level.

And here you are above the object — perhaps you are on a hill or looking down from an upstairs window.

Everyone has their own particular style of sketching—no style can be said to be right or wrong. What can upset a sketch, however, is poor composition and faulty perspective. We have just touched on the basis of perspective and will return to it later. Don't make a problem of it, because it will come naturally to you in time. We are now going to spend some time drawing houses and buildings—but may I suggest that you start with something simple and without too many problems. Here is an old lean-to hut outside my studio. I have drawn it in three stages.

I think I can hear you say: 'That's not all that simple', but in fact it is. You can stop at any stage and it will be a pleasant subject to sketch. Either of these two little pictures could go into your sketch book. Remember how important it is to decide what to leave out. It is all too easy to go on an on until you have spoiled your work with too much detail.

Let me try to convince you that you will have just as much fun sketching smaller details as you will from more complicated set-piece landscape drawings. At this stage choose subjects that are within your ability range. It may be an old shed or a gatepost or a wall, or even a detail from a house. With this more finished sketch I have accentuated parts by shading heavily, and have left other parts relatively light. Remember that shading can create depth.

We will start now with a collection of buildings. You may be in the country or in a town, but the principle is the same. Think from where you would like to sit to do your drawing. You are composing your picture, and I hope using your matchbox or viewer. Try to keep it simple and maybe do one or two light drawings to block in where the outline and rooftops will come. A light line across the page to show the eye level and thus the vanishing points will save you a lot of problems. Here are some step by step stages from a drawing.

Spend a moment or two looking at this drawing. If I had included the granite stone in the end wall of the facing cottage it would have destroyed the feeling of sunlight (which is accentuated by the shadows). The cottage in the distance on the left is brought to life with the shrubs and trees that surround it. The roadway is in sunlight and the boats are a lucky composition bonus. Note that I have only given the barest indication of the granite wall on the right. Finally—there was no need to make any shading in the sky. This is what I mean by deciding what to leave out.

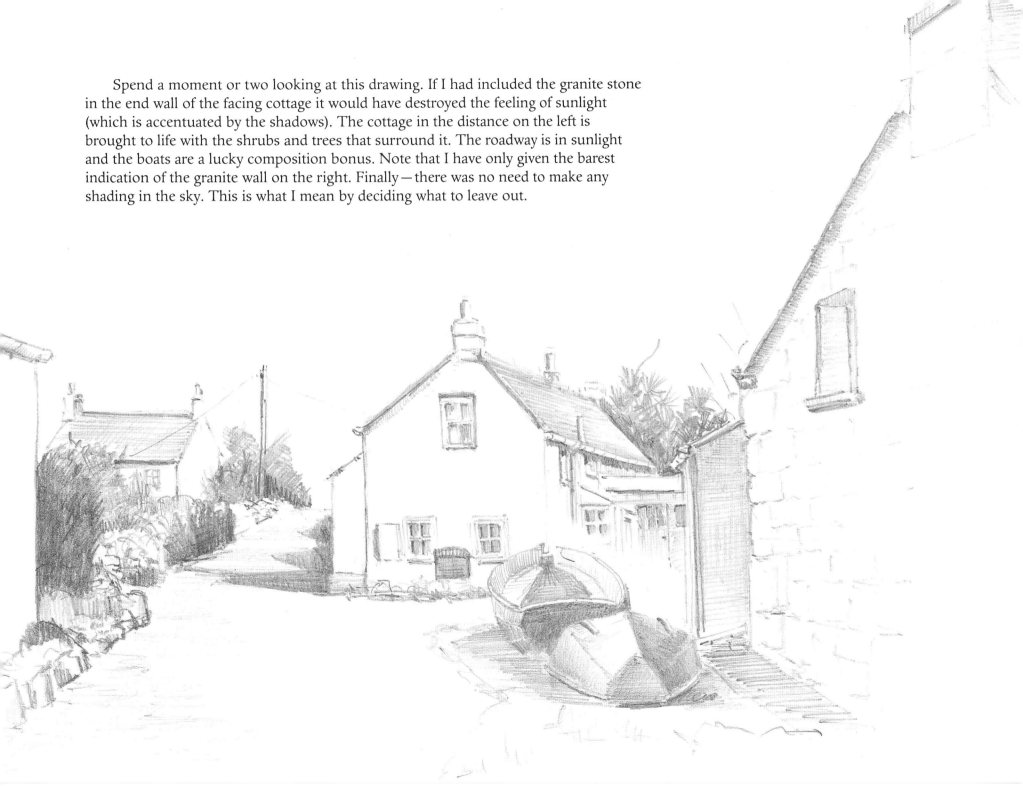

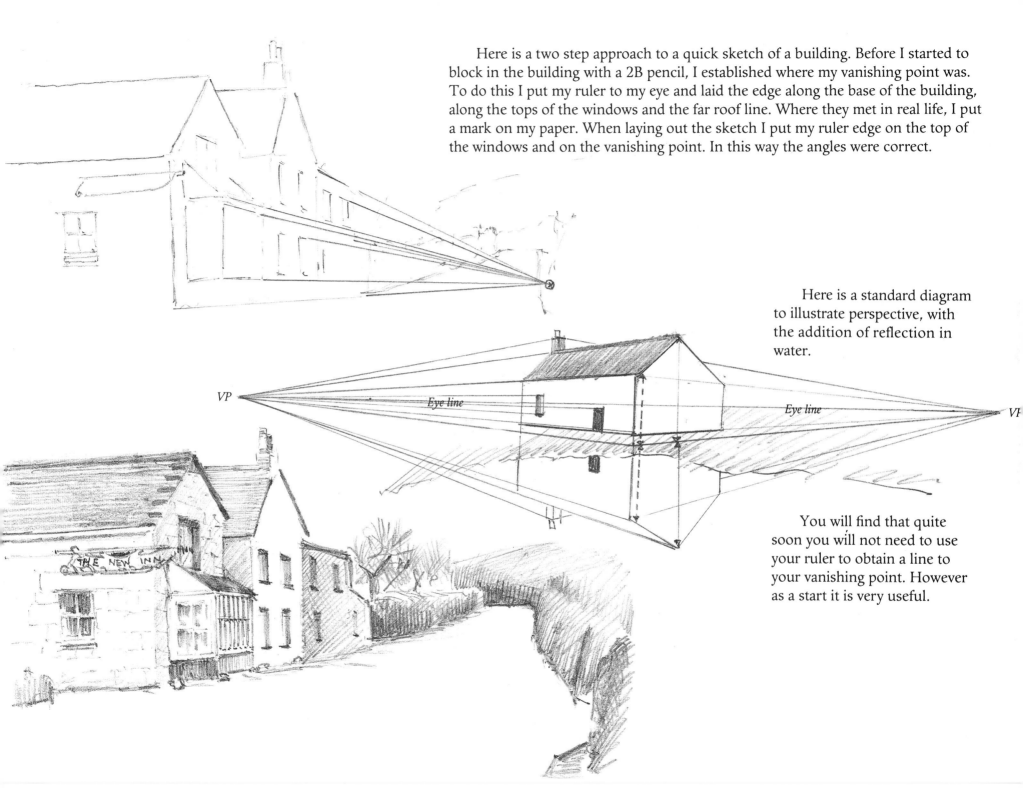

Here is a two step approach to a quick sketch of a building. Before I started to block in the building with a 2B pencil, I established where my vanishing point was. To do this I put my ruler to my eye and laid the edge along the base of the building, along the tops of the windows and the far roof line. Where they met in real life, I put a mark on my paper. When laying out the sketch I put my ruler edge on the top of the windows and on the vanishing point. In this way the angles were correct.

Here is a standard diagram to illustrate perspective, with the addition of reflection in water.

You will find that quite soon you will not need to use your ruler to obtain a line to your vanishing point. However as a start it is very useful.

VP

Eye line

Eye line

VP

Contrasts in shading—
they could both go into your
sketch book, but if you
continued to shade the
left-hand sketch you might
lose some of the lightness.

The collection of barns sketched on the opposite page gives further examples of what to accentuate and what to leave out. The roof of the farmhouse on the left remains in outline only, while the trees behind the cowshed roof are very dark. They push the roofs forward. There is no need to try to draw every branch of the trees. Not only will it be very difficult but it will probably result in them becoming overpowering. Remember that in real life you don't see all the details—it is only when your eye rests on an object that you actually **see** the individual twigs and small branches. In this case you are looking at a scene.

Shading is all important. I think that you will be helped if, as you draw, you fix your thoughts on how you can obtain a feeling of depth three dimensionally. Think to yourself 'I need to bring this part forward, so I must leave the background unshaded for the moment, and accentuate one part so that it stands out'.

Don't worry, it will all come with practice.

This half completed sketch of the other side of the gateway brings out one or two more points. A very light touch with an HB pencil has blocked in the outlines. I used my rubber two or three times before I got the proportions correct. The decision about what to leave out must now be taken. The big fir tree on the left is helping to bring the building forward—but the effect will be lost if we shade the building too much.

How can I get a feeling of distance when looking through the gateway? Possibly either by deep shading inside the gateway and suggesting trees visible on the left through the archway. However I would lose everything if there was too much detail and it became fussy.

Look at this sketch. It is by no means easy when you choose a subject with a number of roof levels. Put your ruler to your eye and lay it along the different lines of the roof. They will converge at a point to the right of the distant cottages. When you start, draw very faint outlines, and don't be afraid to use your rubber until you have got it right. You can then, and only then, build up your shadows.

These little sketches were done during
an afternoon and, while they have no
particular theme, they are good practice
and fun to do.

A word about clouds and the sky. Clouds are fascinating but they can so easily dominate the drawing even if they are not meant to. They can always be built up, so treat them very lightly until you have sensed the correct balance for the picture. We will mention this subject again, but look at the two sketches above. The sketch on the left is rather overbalanced by the strength of the sky.

The one on the right is better I think. However in the sketch on the opposite page the clouds are the dominant feature and the branches of the tree are being blown by the wind. A 6B pencil was used and the whole of the sky shaded in diagonal lines. A touch here and there with my rubber formed the softness of the clouds, then heavier shading strengthened the drawing.

Trees are wonderful subjects for sketching and, having grasped one or two basic ideas, are not too difficult. Light and shade are the whole basis of drawing trees. Unless your eye dwells on a particular tree or clump you will not register much detail, whereas a further glance will take in the branches and finally every twig. This can all be achieved in your drawing. Some people will want to draw with a fine outline and the result will be totally satisfying, while others will seek to use all the pencils in the range. Some will want to put in every detail and some will achieve their results with shading alone. Sunlight and shadow are all important in producing the effect you want. Here are some examples.

And here are some more.

You don't have to move far among trees to find a wealth of subjects, and the pages of your sketch book can be filled with small but very expressive and satisfying individual drawings.

Here are some further examples of trees and branches.

Twigs can be great fun and hugely rewarding.

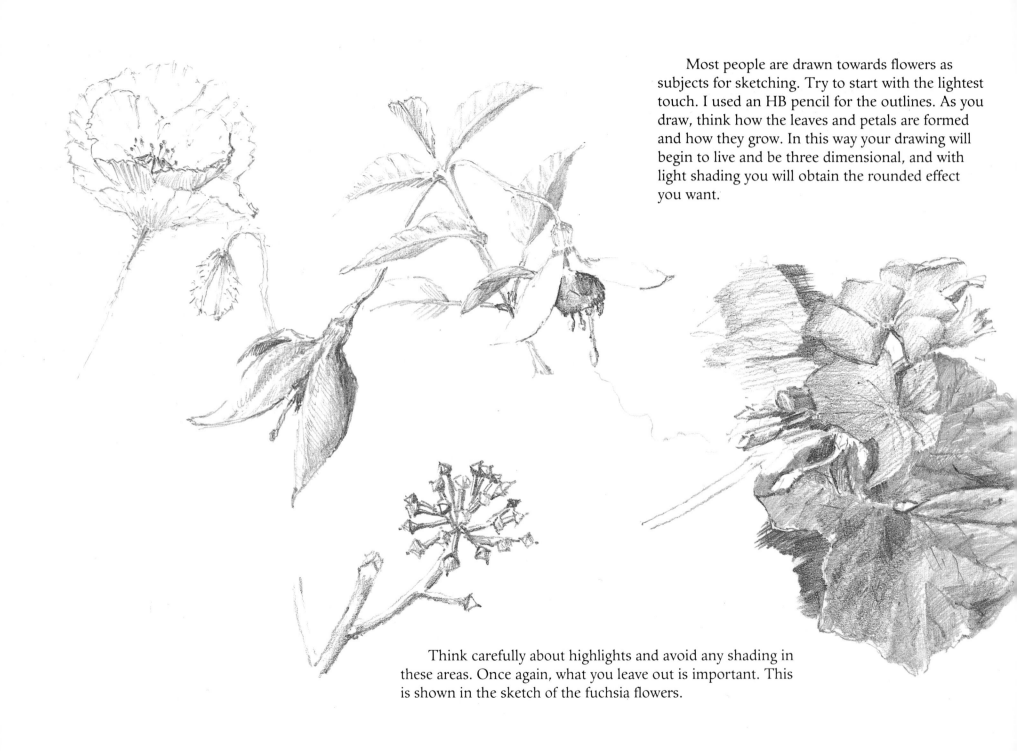

Most people are drawn towards flowers as subjects for sketching. Try to start with the lightest touch. I used an HB pencil for the outlines. As you draw, think how the leaves and petals are formed and how they grow. In this way your drawing will begin to live and be three dimensional, and with light shading you will obtain the rounded effect you want.

Think carefully about highlights and avoid any shading in these areas. Once again, what you leave out is important. This is shown in the sketch of the fuchsia flowers.

The Seashore

Sketching from the beach presents endless possibilities and can give you many hours of enjoyment. Whether it is a view of the harbour or the sand dunes or rocks on the foreshore or even distant islands, the principle is the same.

Decide on your line of horizon.

Set out your vanishing points — if there are buildings.

Remember that you are going to convey a feeling of distance.

Plan your sketch with some small rectangles — decide on the best composition and how much you can fit in (put the cut-out rectangle or matchbox top to your eye).

Make a start by sketching in very lightly the main features, and then strengthen them with some shading. Try to keep the drawing balanced, and get a feeling of distance by outlining features in the horizon very lightly.

I am sure you are going to enjoy yourself, but keep it simple and ensure that your pencils are sharp.

Here is a simple sketch done at low water.

Try to have some of your pages filled with details. It is not only good practice, but it is a delightful reminder of a happy afternoon's sketching. Notice the shading in these sketches. I used a 2B pencil very lightly to draw in the outline and then a 4B. On the next page I have used the pencils to shade in various strokes which give different effects.

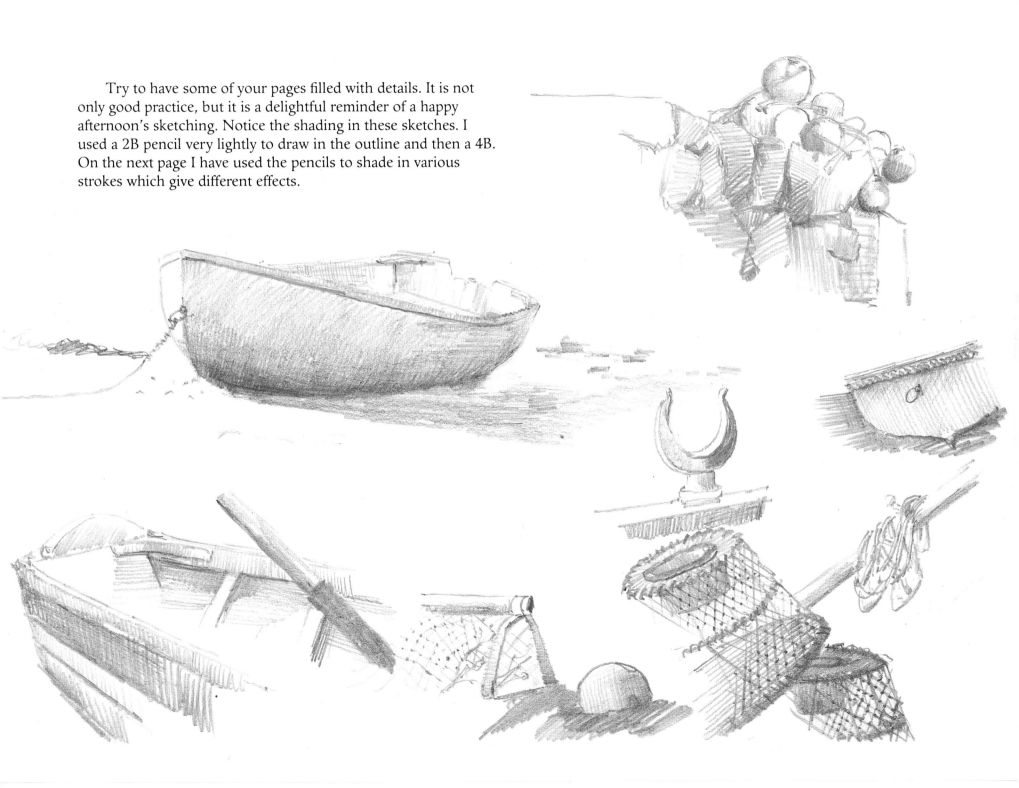

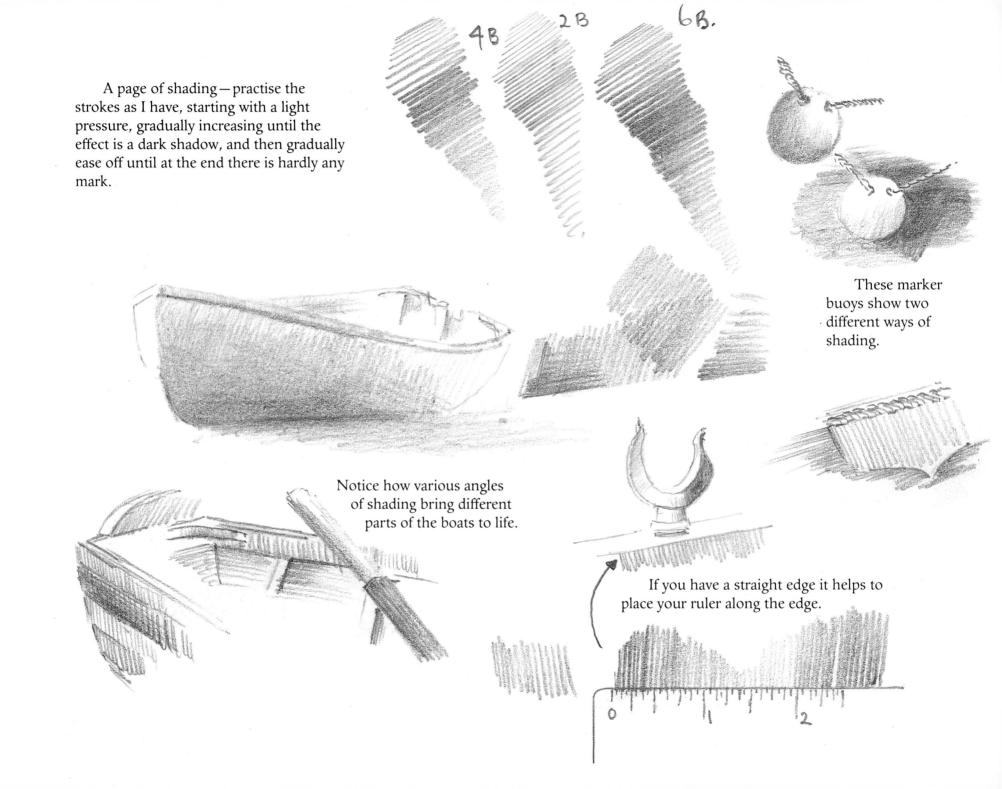

A page of shading—practise the strokes as I have, starting with a light pressure, gradually increasing until the effect is a dark shadow, and then gradually ease off until at the end there is hardly any mark.

4B 2B 6B.

These marker buoys show two different ways of shading.

Notice how various angles of shading bring different parts of the boats to life.

If you have a straight edge it helps to place your ruler along the edge.

0   1   2

I wanted to sketch from where I was sitting, but it wasn't a good composition. There is no obvious focal point which draws your eye (despite an attempt to use birds). I moved a few yards down the beach and the next sketch is more balanced.

The heavily shaded boat in this quick sketch helps to give a feeling of distance.

The direction of the pencil work in this drawing helps to give a feeling of movement.

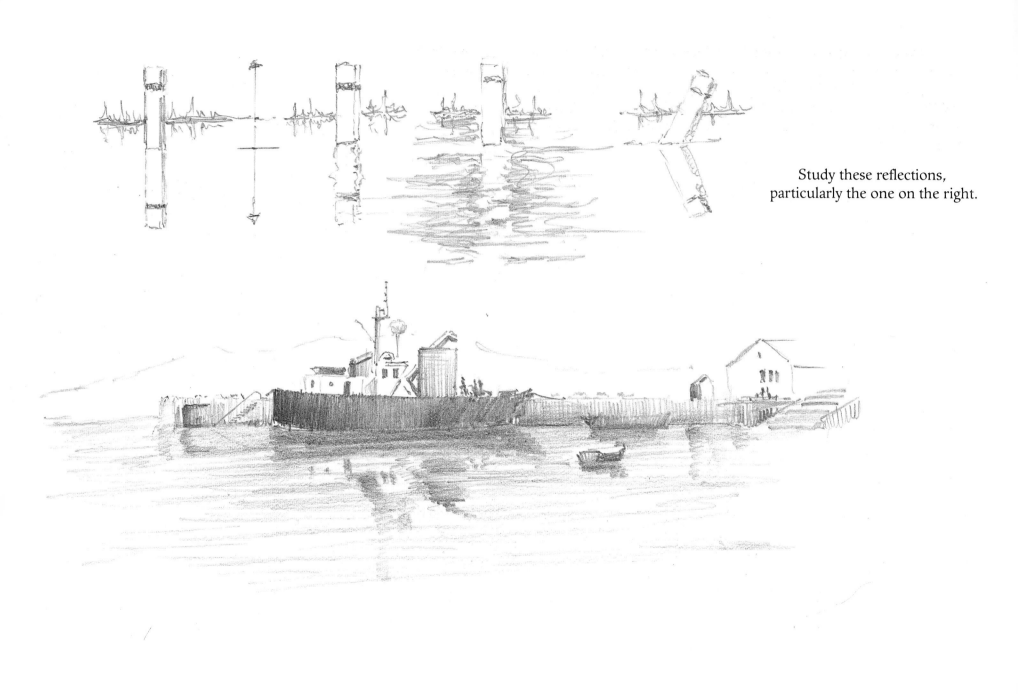

Study these reflections,
particularly the one on the right.

Before starting to sketch still life subjects and the limitless number of objects in the home, you should consider a little bit more about perspective. Here is the simplest explanation, but it will do for now. Just as there is a vanishing point to left and right of the horizon or eye level as we have seen, so there is a vanishing point in a room. Look straight ahead of you and glance at the walls at ceiling height to left and right. You see that they converge.

They do it like this.

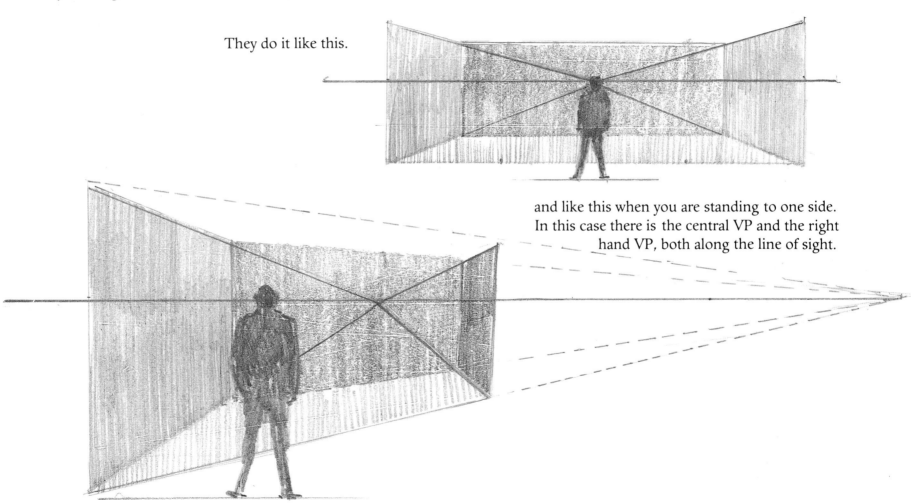

and like this when you are standing to one side. In this case there is the central VP and the right hand VP, both along the line of sight.

I didn't have to move very far in order to fill a page of my sketch book with details in my studio. I used a 6B pencil with a very sharp point and the lightest of touch.

Sitting in the kitchen for an hour produced these little sketches.

Here is a little exercise with still life. Place the objects on a table and shine a light from one side. Don't move them, but walk round the table to find the most attractive composition. Decide how dark you want your finished work to be. My cube became a box and was more attractive with a lighter shade. In this exercise I used 2B and 4B pencils.

When you start a sketch like this use the lightest of touch to draw in the outlines. I used a 2B pencil with a **very** sharp point. My large soft rubber with a straight edge was invaluable. This kind of drawing is not always easy, and if it doesn't appeal to you—don't push it, but stick to subjects in which you feel confident.

Remember—keep your pencils sharp. I had a strip of sandpaper by me and after making a long point with my knife, I used the sandpaper to keep the point sharp.

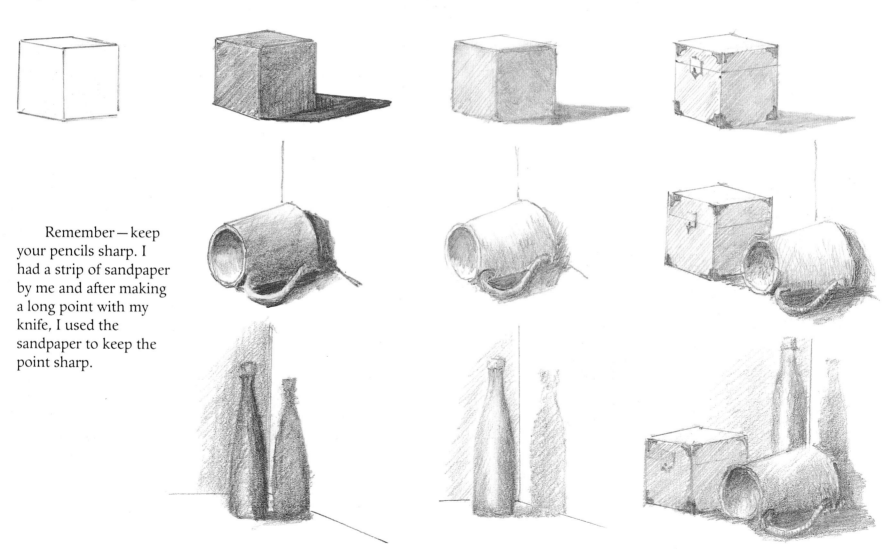

—and here we have another page of little sketches. Not only are they fun to do, they are invaluable in giving you confidence. Don't try too hard, relax and practise using shadows to give you a three dimensional effect.

When tackling this subject, I started by defining the walls and window with a very light touch indeed. To ensure that the light flooded in on to the work bench, I worked outwards from the source of light. It was done with a 2B pencil, and darkened at the bottom with a 6B.